MAR   2004

★ IT'S MY STATE! ★
South Dakota

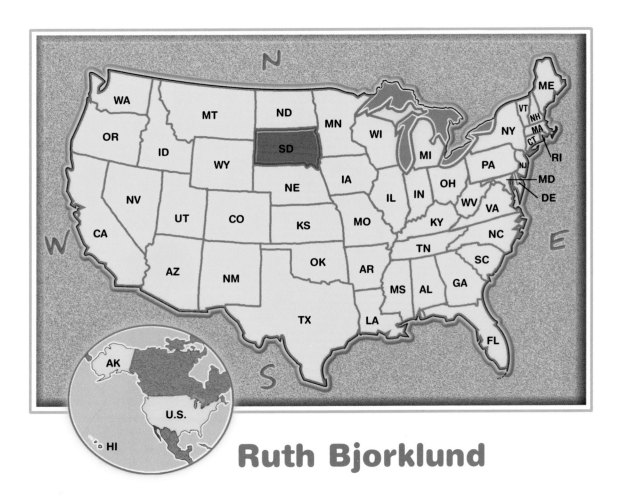

Ruth Bjorklund

BENCHMARK BOOKS

MARSHALL CAVENDISH
NEW YORK

For Marco

Series Consultant

David G. Vanderstel, Ph.D., Executive Director, National Council on Public History

Benchmark Books
Marshall Cavendish
99 White Plains Road
Tarrytown, New York 10591-9001
www.marshallcavendish.com

Text, maps, and illustrations copyright © 2004 by Marshall Cavendish Corporation
Maps and illustrations by Christopher Santoro

Library of Congress Cataloging-in-Publication Data

Bjorklund, Ruth.
South Dakota / by Ruth Bjorklund.
p. cm. — (It's my state!)
Summary: Surveys the history, geography, government, and economy of
South Dakota as well as the diverse ways of life of its people.
Includes bibliographical references and index.
ISBN 0-7614-1531-9
1. South Dakota—Juvenile literature. [1. South Dakota.]
I. Title. II. Series.

F651.3.B58 2004
978.3—dc21
2003000126

Photo research by Candlepants, Inc.

Cover photograph: Digital Vision / Getty Images, Inc.

Back cover illustration: The license plate shows South Dakota's postal abbreviation, followed by its year of statehood.

The photographs in this book are used by permission and through the courtesy of: *Corbis:* 32, 36; Frank Young / Papilio, 4 (top); Joe McDonald, 4 (middle); W. Perry Conway, 5 (middle), 19 (top); Michael S. Yamashita, 5 (bottom); Phil Schermeister, 12; Ron Sanford, 16; Richard Hamilton Smith, 18 (middle); Bettmann, 22, 31, 39 (top), 51 (bottom); Historical Picture Archive, 29; Minnesota Historical Society, 33; Underwood & Underwood, 35; AFP, 38, 51 (top); Philip Gould, 39 (bottom); Becky Luigart-Stayner, 45; John-Marshall Mantel, 50 (middle); Trapper Frank, 50 (bottom); Ralph A. Clevenger, 68 (middle); Layne Kennedy, 68 (bottom); Lester Lefkowitz, 69 (bottom); Annie Griffiths Belt, 70. *Animals Animals / Earth Scenes:* Ted Levin, 18 (bottom); Paul Berquist, 19 (bottom). *Getty Images, Inc.:* Glen Allison / PhotoDisc, 11, 59; Stone, 56. *Bill Lindner Photography:* 5 (top). *Minden Pictures:* Jim Brandenburg, 17, 21. *PeopleScapes / Greg Latza:* 4 (bottom), 8, 10, 14, 18 (top), 19 (middle), 20, 40, 43, 44, 46, 47, 48, 49, 52, 54, 55, 62, 64, 66, 67, 68 (top), 69 (top), 69 (middle), 71, 73, 74. *Art Resource, NY:* Smithsonian American Art Museum, Washington, DC, 25. *Bridgeman Art Library:* Thomas Mickell Burnham, Private Collection, 28. *Chicago Historical Society (P and S 1928.00690):* 50 (top). *Courtesy of Ms. Beulah Campbell:* 51 (middle).

Book design by Anahid Hamparian

Printed in Italy

1   3   5   6   4   2

Contents

A Quick Look at South Dakota

Nickname: The Mount Rushmore State

Population: 754,844 (2000)

Statehood: 1889

Flower: Pasque Flower

The pasque flower blooms in the early spring, often before the snow melts. This pale lavender wildflower may look delicate, but it is a hardy plant common to the northern prairie and the Great Plains.

Bird:

Ring-Necked Pheasant

Ring-necked pheasants look like chickens with long tails. Males are brightly colored in red, gold, and green with a white ring around their necks. Females are more drab and brownish. These seed-eating birds live near wheat and cornfields and make their nests in the state's vast grasslands.

Tree: Black Hills Spruce

The Black Hills spruce is a type of evergreen. The tree is cone shaped with dark blue-green needles. The Black Hills region is covered with so many of these trees that the hills appear black from a distance. That is how the area got its name.

Fish: Walleye

The walleye is a torpedo-shaped fish that likes cold, fresh water. Known for its good night vision, the fish can hunt for food in almost total darkness. South Dakota's fishermen know that the best times to catch a walleye are at dawn and at dusk when the light is dim.

Animal: Coyote

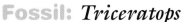

Called "prairie wolves" by explorers Lewis and Clark, coyotes can be found across the state. They are fast-moving creatures that live in packs and mate for life. They use loud howls and playful yips to communicate with each other.

Fossil: Triceratops

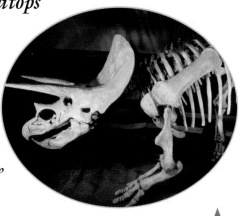

In prehistoric times, the plant-eating Triceratops roamed across the region that is now the Great Plains. This dinosaur weighed as much as 6 tons and had a bony ruffle called a frill around its head. It also had two 3-foot-long horns on its brow and a long snout. Its name means "three-horned face."

SOUTH DAKOTA

Aberdeen

Black Hills National Forest

Deadwood

Rapid City

Cheyenne River

Lake Oahe

Badlands National Park

White River

Pierre

De Smet

Brookings

James River

Mitchell

Sioux Falls

Harney Peak

Mount Rushmore National Memorial

Wounded Knee

Pine Ridge

Little White River

Yankton

Vermillion

Big Sioux River

Missouri River

N

W   E

S

1 The Mount Rushmore State

South Dakota is known as the Mount Rushmore State. If you think about its other nicknames, the Sunshine State and the Coyote State, you still may not have a clear picture of what the state is all about. Yes, the sun shines more than two hundred days each year, but the wind blows, lightning strikes, and rain falls. Coyotes do wander about the state, but they roam alongside deer, prairie dogs, and growing herds of pronghorn antelope and buffalo. And as for being known for its most famous tourist attraction, South Dakota offers much more—ancient history and fossil sites, rich traditional cultures, dramatic mountains, grasslands, caves, and two national parks. No single nickname can really do South Dakota justice. At times, the state has been called the Land of Infinite Variety, which might just be the best description of all.

South Dakota's Borders
North: North Dakota
South: Nebraska
East: Minnesota and Iowa
West: Montana and Wyoming

Prairies, Potholes, Badlands, and Buttes

If you and three other friends each lived at one of the farthest corners of the United States and wanted to meet in the country's exact middle, you would gather on a lonely piece of prairie seventeen miles west of Castle Rock, South Dakota. At the geographic center of the country, South Dakota is where east meets west.

South Dakota's landscape changes as you travel from east to west. When the Ice Age glaciers grew and shrank, they dragged rocks and debris across the land in the northeastern part of the state. The glaciers also created hills pitted with small lakes and ponds, called "prairie potholes." In 1839,

In spring, the rolling prairie turns a brilliant green.

French mapmaker Joseph Nicollet described the area as "beautiful to the eyes." Today, hawks, eagles, owls, and hundreds of other birds and ducks continue to flock to these bodies of water. Trees, such as maple, ironwood, chokecherry, and box elder thrive here, as well as wildflowers of almost every color.

In southeastern South Dakota, tall prairie grasses added nutrients to the soil for more than ten thousand years. There you will find rolling fields ripe with corn, soybeans, oats, and wheat. Much of South Dakota's population lives in the eastern part of the state, in cities such as Sioux Falls and Brookings, or on nearby farms. Rivers and streams flow through the region. Willow and cottonwood trees line the banks of many of the rivers and streams. Pheasant, waterfowl, and deer make their homes among these trees.

The Missouri River, known as the "Big Muddy," divides South Dakota nearly in half. Up until two hundred years ago, the constantly shifting river was the heart of a huge valley. It was filled with vast herds of bison, bear, elk, wolves, bighorn sheep, whooping cranes, and other wildlife. Today, dams built to improve agriculture and commerce have turned the river into a series of four large lakes, or reservoirs. Little of the river has been left to run wild and little of the original wildlife remains. In some areas, however, it is still possible to spot birds, such as blackbirds, flickers, and pheasant. Ducks, geese, deer, and coyote are also still around the areas.

If you cross the Missouri River in South Dakota you had better reset the time on your watch. Eastern South Dakota is in the Central Time Zone, while western South Dakota follows Mountain Time.

Meriwether Lewis climbed the hills overlooking the Missouri River and wrote that the scenery was "rich, pleasing, and beautiful."

In the region now known as South Dakota, Ice Age glaciers did not spread west of the Missouri River. More than seventy million years ago, western South Dakota was once the floor of an ancient sea. Layers of rock, clay, sand, silt, and other debris settled there. Over time as the seas dried, wind and water wore down the layers into different shapes. These layers contain an important record of prehistoric life, making South Dakota one of the best places to study fossils. More than 5,000 bones have been found at the site known as the Big Pig Dig in Badlands National Park, where the remains of ancient horses, dogs, saber-toothed cats, rhinoceros, and deer have been uncovered.

West of the Missouri River, the land rises and becomes drier and less populated. In this area there are ranches and a few remote farms. Short grasses such as blue grama and buffalo grass sprout for miles. Farther west, sharp spires of rock and clay form an area called the Badlands. In 1839, Catholic missionary Father Pierre-Jean De Smet wrote that the badlands, from a distance, looked like "ancient castles." Folded, twisted, and difficult to travel through, the badlands are covered in brush and grass, prickly-pear cactus, yucca, and sage. They are also home to many creatures such as rattlesnakes, eagles, prairie dogs, rabbits, pronghorn antelope, and bison. Much of the soil west of the Missouri River is a hard, red adobe clay called "gumbo." When it rains, it becomes slick and gooey. Most country roads are made of this sticky mixture, and smart locals know when and how to avoid getting stuck.

Fossils dating back 23 to 35 million years are only some of the natural riches of Badlands National Park.

The variety of landscapes in the Black Hills ranges from sparkling rivers and deep canyons to granite peaks and grasslands.

Southwest of the Badlands is another South Dakota natural treasure—the Black Hills. These ancient mountains were formed of magma, or liquid rock, stored deep in the earth, close to one billion years ago. The hills, sacred to the area's Native American tribes, are ninety million years older than the Rocky Mountains. The Lakota named them Paha Sapa, which means "hills that are black." Giant granite peaks and deep canyons add to the beauty. Trees such as oak, ash, willow, and aspen can be found there. A wealth of

In South Dakota's Badlands National Park, rock hounds can find an interesting volcanic rock called cinder rock. When it was formed, cinder rock hardened while lava was still boiling. Because it is so full of bubbles, a chunk of cinder rock can float in water.

wildflowers is also present. These include prairie coneflower, black-eyed Susan, larkspur, lady slipper, and primrose. Deer, wild turkey, and elk live in the woodlands. The high ridges and lush meadows nearby are home to growing herds of bison, golden and bald eagles, coyote, beaver, mountain goats, porcupines, prairie dogs, bobcats, and mountain lions.

On a granite cliff in the Black Hills in 1927, sculptor Gutzon Borglum began carving 60-foot-high faces of four United States presidents. The faces of Presidents Washington, Jefferson, Lincoln, and Theodore Roosevelt are on the 5,725-foot mountain memorial known as Mount Rushmore.

Some of the wonders of this region are below the ground. Limestone caves line the area, complete with cone-shaped rock formations and frost crystals.

Climate

The seasons differ sharply in South Dakota. In 1936, for example, temperatures went from a winter low of minus 58 degrees Fahrenheit to a summer high of 120 degrees. That is a record-breaking difference of 177 degrees in one year! On average, summer temperatures are 70 degrees, but 100-degree days are fairly common. Humidity, or moisture in the air, is generally low, so residents claim that the hot, dry heat is bearable. Spring and fall feature pleasant temperatures from the 60s to the low 80s.

Winter blizzards blast residents with fierce winds, blinding snow, and arctic temperatures. On an average, 18 inches of rain and snow fall each year. The northwest receives about 14 inches. Approximately 25 inches falls in the southeast. Most precipitation in South Dakota falls as rain.

A common sight over the prairie, the average lightning bolt is 6 to 8 miles long.
It can travel 25 to 40 miles across the sky before striking the ground.

South Dakota

In spring, the rains can come hard and often, flooding the plains and damaging homes, towns, crops, and roadways. In the winter and early spring, South Dakota, along with other northwestern states, can be affected by the Chinook winds. These warm, dry winds blow along the Rocky Mountains, warming as they move to lower elevations. On January 23, 1943, windows in the town of Spearfish broke when a Chinook wind caused the temperature to rise 49 degrees in just two minutes. At 7:30 A.M. the temperature was an icy 4 degrees below zero, but by 7:32 A.M., it was 45 degrees above.

In the summer, thunderstorms are sudden and often violent. They can carry harmful hail, rain, lightning, and winds that can gust fifty to one hundred miles per hour. According to the National Weather Service in Sioux Falls, a single prairie thunderstorm can deliver fifty thousand lightning strikes. "There was something savage and terrifying in the howling yellow swallowing the sky," wrote Rose Wilder Lane, daughter of author Laura Ingalls Wilder.

Prairie Wildlife

The fossil sites throughout the state show that the prairie has long been home to a wide variety of creatures. From the earliest *Tyrannosaurus rex* to the present-day coyote, wildlife has thrived in South Dakota's prairie potholes, badlands, rivers, grasslands, and Black Hills.

In 1804, explorer Meriwether Lewis climbed a hill along the Missouri River and as he looked below, he wrote that he saw buffalo, elk, deer, and antelope "feeding in every direction. . . ." Together with his fellow explorer, William Clark, Lewis took note of hundreds of grassland animals living on America's prairies.

Custer State Park is home to the second-largest public buffalo herd in the country.

Lewis and Clark were so charmed by prairie dogs, which they called "barking squirrels," that they sent a live one to Washington, D.C., as a gift for President Thomas Jefferson

The land had animals such as grizzly bears, buffalo, prairie dogs, bighorn sheep, coyote, prairie chickens, and black-footed ferrets. The settlers who later came to farm the plains drove many of these creatures away. At one time, 70 million buffalo roamed the prairie. By 1883, the buffalo was nearly extinct. Today, there are herds of buffalo at Wind Cave and Badlands National Parks, Custer State Park, Buffalo Gap National Grasslands, Black Hills National Forest, and many private ranches. The largest buffalo herd in the United States is on the Standing Butte Ranch near Pierre, South Dakota.

Buffalo or bison? The scientific name for the animal we know as the American buffalo is *Bison bison*. Some people refer to the animals as bison, while many more use the more familiar term buffalo.

Plants & Animals

Golden Eagle

Golden eagles are large birds of prey with gold feathers on their heads, sharp talons, and hooked beaks. They soar over open fields, using their huge eyes to spot prey. A golden eagle can spy a rabbit from more than a mile away.

Coneflower

Purple and yellow coneflowers grow well in the extreme climate of the prairie. Native Americans used the roots of this plant to make a tea to cure sore throats, snake bites, and colds. The popular remedy now known as echinacea (eck-uh-NAY-sha) comes from purple coneflowers.

Buffalo Grass

Buffalo grass has short stems and grows all over the Great Plains. Native people once used the grass for basket weaving and its berries for dye. Today it is still a favorite food of buffalo.

Pronghorn Antelope

For more than a million years, the pronghorn has roamed the Great Plains. Able to run up to 70 miles an hour, the pronghorn is one of the fastest mammals in the world. Settlement of the West nearly killed off this creature, but today, the pronghorn population is growing.

Cottonwood Tree

Cottonwood trees, with their puffy white seeds and shimmering leaves, were a welcome sight for pioneers. Homesteaders discovered early that the tree could thrive on the plains, so they planted them for fuel, shade, timber, and protection from the wind.

Western Hognose Snake

The western hognose snake is also known as the puff adder or hissing adder. Though it hisses when frightened, the hognose is not venomous. It will even try to play dead when a human is near. The hognose hunts for salamanders, toads, frogs, worms, insects, and spiders by using its pointed snout to dig in the dirt.

A biologist releases a black-footed ferret. It is one of the most endangered mammals in North America.

At the time Lewis and Clark passed through South Dakota, nearly 20 percent of the land was covered in prairie dog towns. Prairie dogs loosen the soil when they dig their underground tunnels. Farmers thought they were pests and over time tried to rid the land of them. But in doing so they also harmed the black-footed ferret, which lived in prairie dog towns and hunted prairie dogs at night. Because the ferret's food source had shrunk, experts thought the ferrets had disappeared. But one day in 1981, a rancher's dog returned home with a black-footed ferret it had caught. Some had survived! Today, this clever hunter is on the federal endangered species list. National Forest and National Park Service workers have brought black-footed ferrets into protected prairie dog towns in

Badlands National Park and Buffalo Gap National Grasslands. They hope that the ferrets will once again make the areas their homes.

For ages, hundreds of species of birds and ducks have made their nests in the prairie wetlands. However, in the past century, most of the wetlands have been changed into farmland. Concerned citizens and government agencies are working to preserve the remaining wetlands for future generations of teal, cormorants, grebes, Canada and snow geese, pelicans, herons, cranes, swans, hawks, and eagles. Wildlife refuges have been set up, and many farmers have agreed not to disturb nests or pools of standing water until after the mating season. By working together, rangers, environmentalists, and the concerned citizens of South Dakota are helping to protect and preserve many of North America's native animals.

> *Animals are part of us . . . the winged and four-legged are our cousins. . . . There is power in the buffalo. There is power in the antelope. There was great power in a wolf, even in a coyote. To us, life, all life, is sacred.*
> —John Fire Lame Deer, Lakota

These ferruginous hawks, need wilderness to thrive. A favorite nesting spot is the prairie pothole region.

2 From the Beginning

An Oglala Sioux holy man named Black Elk once said, "The Power of the World always works in circles." You can see the passage of time in the land we know as South Dakota. From 65 million years ago when dinosaurs such as *T. rex* ruled the land to the present day when the bones of a dinosaur named Sue were discovered, the state has taken a dramatic march through the ages.

The First People

About ten thousand years ago, Paleo-Indians moved into the area now known as South Dakota. Their ancestors had crossed a land bridge from Asia into North America. They were following bison, ground sloths, mammoths, and other large mammals. They hunted these animals using spears with sharp stone points. When the climate changed, the large animals died off. The Paleo-Indians then turned to fishing, hunting smaller creatures, and gathering nuts and berries.

A family living on a farm in Miller, South Dakota, in 1936

23

People known as Mound Builders followed the Paleo-Indians and moved into eastern South Dakota. Like the Paleo-Indians, the Mound Builders fished and hunted small game and gathered nuts and berries. They also built villages along the rivers, where they formed large dirt mounds to bury and honor their dead. Archaeologists who have studied the Mound Builder sites in South Dakota have found ancient pottery, stone tools, and decorative beads made from shells.

Allies and Enemies

In the sixteenth century, the Arikara, or Ree, Indians followed the Missouri River into what is now South Dakota. They were villagers, traders, and farmers who grew corn, beans, and squash. Nomadic tribes such as the Cheyenne, Pawnee, and Crow also moved into the area. The Arikaras traded their horses and extra food for buffalo meat, skins, and fur robes.

To the east, in the region now known as Minnesota, French trappers lived among the Ojibwa (or Chippewa) tribe. The French traded guns and tools for the Ojibwa's beaver pelts. The guns gave the Ojibwa power over their Native American enemies, mainly the Dakota. The Ojibwa called the Dakota *Nadouéssioux*, meaning "Little Snakes." The French shortened the name to Sioux. The Dakota, or Sioux, were forced west. They soon divided into three groups: the Dakota Sioux stayed in western Minnesota, the Nakota settled in eastern South Dakota, and the Lakota went west beyond the Missouri River.

In Ojibwa territory, the Sioux had been woodland dwellers who hunted only small animals and collected nuts and berries. But once the Sioux began living in Arikara territory, they learned about horses. This changed their way of life. After becoming horsemen, the Sioux turned out to be skilled buffalo hunters and expert warriors. They also started living in portable homes called tipis. These cone-shaped dwellings stood on wooden poles and were covered with animal hides. The Sioux built their tipis at a slight angle. Because of the angle, their homes could catch cool breezes in the summer. In the winter, the tipis could be turned away from the cold winds. The Sioux took pride in their tipis and often painted them with religious symbols.

Artist George Catlin traveled "into the heart of the buffalo country" and painted scenes of life on the Great Plains. In his journal, he reported that the Indians of the Upper Missouri lived in "a country well-stocked with buffaloes."

Making a Winter Count

The Lakota Indians who lived on the Plains kept a timeline of their history called a Winter Count. They counted years by counting winters. A winter started with the first snowfall of the year. Each year, the elders of the tribe selected the most important event and the Keeper of the Count painted that event onto an animal hide. Traditional Winter Counts were painted in a spiral shape, with the key event in the center, and all the rest flowing out and around in a spiral. In later years, the Lakota used paper and sometimes painted the Winter Count in rows from left to right. By following these instructions, you can make your own Winter Count.

What You Need

Newspaper, plastic sheeting, or other table protection
Piece of black or brown vinyl, 12 by 18 inches (available in fabric stores), or a
    large sheet of construction paper
Scissors
Scrap paper
Pen or pencil
Acrylic paints
Paintbrushes
Jar of water

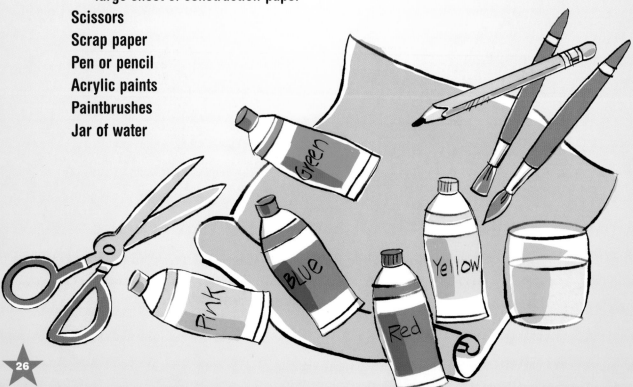

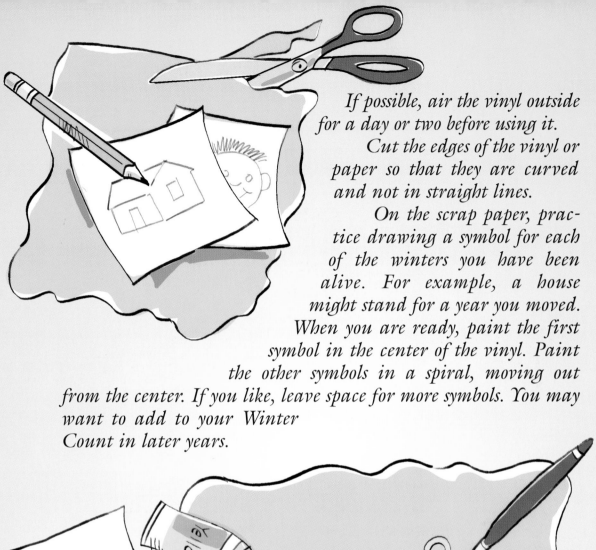

If possible, air the vinyl outside for a day or two before using it.

Cut the edges of the vinyl or paper so that they are curved and not in straight lines.

On the scrap paper, practice drawing a symbol for each of the winters you have been alive. For example, a house might stand for a year you moved. When you are ready, paint the first symbol in the center of the vinyl. Paint the other symbols in a spiral, moving out from the center. If you like, leave space for more symbols. You may want to add to your Winter Count in later years.

The First Europeans

As early as 1540, Europeans had ventured into what is now the American West. The first Europeans to explore the region that is now South Dakota were two French-Canadian brothers, François and Louis-Joseph La Vérendrye. In 1743, they claimed the territory for the king of France and inscribed their names on a lead plate that they buried on top of a hill. The plate went undiscovered for 170 years. A great deal happened during those years. During the eighteenth century, most outsiders had not yet moved into the region and the culture of the Plains Indians thrived. Food, in the form of buffalo, was plentiful. The Native Americans had few enemies.

The plains were part of an area west of the Mississippi River known as the Louisiana Territory. In Europe, the Louisiana Territory changed ownership from France to Spain and back to France. In 1803, President Thomas Jefferson bought the

Meriwether Lewis and William Clark explore the land along the Missouri River.

territory from France. This purchase doubled the size of the young American nation. Right away, President Jefferson commissioned two U.S. Army officers, Meriwether Lewis and William Clark, to explore the new land. In 1804, Lewis and Clark and their party traveled along the Missouri River and visited several Native American villages and camps. For the most part, their meetings were friendly.

In 1817, Joseph La Framboise established the first permanent white settlement near Fort Pierre. Soon others followed. The first steamboat up the Missouri, the *Yellowstone*, was a great aid in bringing trappers to the wilderness. The boat was also used to ship their goods to eastern markets. The trappers' interest in the area ended by the mid-1800s, however, once most of the beaver were gone. But as the trappers moved on, East Coast farmers came fast on their heels in search of land. The new settlers were taking over and farming Indian land, angering many native leaders. The Plains Indians were unwilling to give up the "land of their

This painting shows Fort Pierre on the Missouri River.

fathers" without a fight. As Teton Sioux chief Sitting Bull explained, "When I was a boy, the Sioux owned the world. The sun rose and set on their land. . . . If we must die, we die defending our rights." The newcomers also killed nearly all the buffalo. This cut the Indians off from their greatest source of food, clothing, and shelter.

The clashes between Indians and settlers persuaded many pioneers to turn back. But the U.S. government wanted whites to settle the newly named Dakota Territory. Officials signed the Fort Laramie Treaty of 1868, which formed the Great Sioux Reservation west of the Missouri River. It gave the land to the tribes and did not allow whites to enter. The Yankton Sioux, from southeastern South Dakota, was one group that agreed to move to a reservation to make way for pioneer farmers. The Civil War had ended three years earlier. With the end of the war and the new treaties, people felt more at ease moving west to the Dakota Territory.

However, as white settlers passed through the overland trails of South Dakota, Native American leaders such as Crazy Horse and Sitting Bull tried to resist their advances. Red Cloud, a Lakota chief, led many battles against whites entering the Black Hills. He declared, "We did not ask you white men to come here. The Great Spirit gave us this country as a home. You had yours."

In 1874, relations between whites and Native Americans reached a boiling point when Army general George Custer discovered a treasure in the Black Hills—gold. He spread the word quickly and gold seekers from across the continent soon arrived in the hopes of mining the Black Hills. Almost overnight, the rough-and-tumble Black Hills mining towns of Deadwood and

South Dakota

Lead became a magnet for adventurers, including Calamity Jane, Wild Bill Hickok, and the famous black cowboy Nat Love.

Most Native Americans in the area were not pleased. The Sioux wanted to protect their sacred lands, but the U.S. government violated the treaty by starving out the Sioux and taking control of the territory that had been granted to them. Red Cloud described the government's actions. "They made us many promises, more than I can remember, but they never kept but one; they promised to take our land, and they took it."

At Wounded Knee Creek, in December 1890, the U.S. Cavalry surrounded a cold, hungry, and defenseless band of Indians. When a shot rang out, the soldiers responded with gun and cannon fire that killed hundreds of men, women, and

Government troops are shown firing on Plains Indians at the Battle at Wounded Knee Creek.

children. This massacre was the final chapter in the war between the Plains Indians and the U.S. government. Many Plains Indians had no choice but to give up their lands. As Black Elk lamented, "A people's dream died there."

Carving the Frontier

Anxious to expand the nation, the U.S. government had passed the Homestead Act in 1862. This act of Congress offered 160 acres of land to any person willing to pay a small filing fee and live and work on the land for five years. The nation was growing and changing. Railroads were being built. To speed their progress, railroad officials advertised heavily in Europe. They posted flyers that promised, "Best Wheat Lands, Best Farming Lands, Best Grazing Lands in the world. . . . FREE TO ALL!"

A wagon train loaded with freight travels through the Black Hills in 1887.

Soon Swedes, Germans, Russians, Czechs, Norwegians, and Danes were joining the ranks of the pioneers headed for the Dakota Territory.

Often, the first task for these pioneers was to build a house. The plains had few, if any, trees, so the farmers were forced to build with the hard-packed pieces of earth called sod. They plowed the heavy top layer of sod in long strips that they cut into building blocks. Whole families stacked the heavy sod blocks on top of one another, making walls and leaving openings for windows and a door. The houses were called soddies. These homes stayed warm in winter and cool in summer because of the dirt roofs and walls. They were not perfect homes by any means. Many irritations came through the walls—rain, dust, snakes, rodents, and even an occasional cow walking across a low-lying roof.

Farming the plains was not a simple task. Drought was a constant threat, as were storms, prairie fires, frost, and destructive pests such as grasshoppers. Most homesteaders left their claims

This farmer and his family stand outside of their sodhouse around 1880.

and moved on. Laura Ingalls Wilder was part of a home-steading family in De Smet, South Dakota. Wilder and her husband, Almanzo Wilder, lasted longer than most before giving up. Their daughter, Rose, wrote, "It was a saying in the Dakotas that the Government bet . . . that the land would starve a man out in less than five years. My father won that bet. It took seven successive years of complete crop failure . . . to dislodge us from that land."

Statehood

Despite the hardships, there were enough farmers, ranchers, railroad workers, and miners in 1889 to qualify the Dakota Territory for statehood. Residents of the Dakotas believed statehood would give them pride, identity, government jobs, and other benefits. On November 2, 1889, President Grover Cleveland signed documents making North Dakota and South Dakota the thirty-ninth and fortieth states of the Union. Pierre was named South Dakota's capital because it was the closest town to the geographic center of the state.

Statehood brought little change to the day-to-day lives of South Dakotans. The state remained a difficult place to make a living. But a decade or so into the twentieth century, fortunes changed. During most of the time between 1910 until the end of World War I, weather was good and crops thrived. When the world went to war in 1914, South Dakotans answered the government's call. Thirty-two thousand young men and women enlisted to serve in the military while others stayed home on the farm, raising wheat, corn, and livestock to feed the rest of the nation. Patriotic posters encouraged farmers to "Sow the Seeds of Victory!"

After winning the war, with enthusiasm still high, South Dakotans decided to build a monument that would attract visitors and tourist dollars to the state. They turned to a sculptor named Gutzon Borglum, who chose a granite mountain in the Black Hills to carve a memorial to the nation. With the help of more

Gutzon Borglum works on a model of an early version of the Mount Rushmore memorial.

than four hundred craftsmen, he began blasting the granite of Mount Rushmore and carving in stone the faces of Presidents Washington, Jefferson, Lincoln, and Theodore Roosevelt. On the day work began, President Calvin Coolidge declared the sculpture would be "a picture of hope fulfilled." Mount Rushmore was completed in 1941.

Dusty Old Dust

Hopeful miners gave their claims upbeat names such as "Golden Slipper Mine" or "Jackpot Mine," while other names such as "Dead Broke Mine" or "Hardscrabble Mine" told another story. This mixture of hardship and success was a common experience for all South Dakotans, farmers and miners alike. The farmers, in their eagerness to supply the nation with food during the war years, had plowed up too much sod. After World War I, the rains stopped coming. By the 1930s, droughts had taken their toll. Without healthy crops or native grasses to

In 1936 a dust storm buried the farm machinery on this farm in Dallas, South Dakota.

hold down the sod, the dry, lifeless soil simply blew away. Great swirls of black dust blanketed the plains.

The dust bowl days were part of the era known as the Great Depression. Throughout the nation, people were looking for work and many families were going hungry. During the 1930s the federal government created programs to help these families. Some federal money was used to create new housing. The government also planted many trees in certain areas to block the dusty winds. Farmers learned more about protecting the soil and eventually the land became useful again.

The United States entered World War II in 1941. Going to war helped end many of the country's economic troubles. South Dakota farmers and ranchers grew food to feed the nation and the world. Many South Dakotans worked in factories that built supplies for the war effort.

On the Home Front

After World War II, South Dakota turned once again to its own needs. Cities slowly grew, creating new and different kinds of jobs. The federal government built four large dams on the Missouri River. The dams provided hydroelectric power—energy created by the flow of water—flood control, and irrigation for crops. The government also built Army Air Corps bases, one in western

South Dakota, which became Ellsworth Air Force Base, and others in the eastern part of the state. In each of these areas, the number of science and technology jobs increased. Technology then spread to the world of farming. Today's farmers use computers and scientific instruments to do many tasks. These tasks include measuring seeds and water, destroying harmful insects, and saving crops from spoiling.

But prosperity has come slowly, if at all, to many of South Dakota's poorest residents, the Native Americans. Many were forced onto reservations with weak soils and have been poorly served by government programs. It has been hard for the members of South Dakota's tribes to replace their early way of life. Serious problems with poverty, alcoholism, and unemployment occur on the reservations. In the 1960s, many Sioux decided that the time for change had come. An organization was formed called the American Indian Movement (AIM), led by Russell Means of the Pine Ridge Reservation. The movement's main goal was to show the rest of the country and the world the injustices endured by Native Americans. Means led a demonstration at the site where the Wounded Knee Massacre had taken place. He and his fellow Lakota Sioux protested the conditions of the nation's reservations. This included the breaking of treaties—especially the Fort Laramie Treaty, which had given the Black Hills to the Lakota "forever"—and the government's poor handling of Indian-owned funds and investments. For seventy-one days, AIM members held off federal agents until the government at last agreed to discuss the Fort Laramie Treaty. On March 24, 1980, the Supreme Court case called *United States* v. *Sioux Nation of Indians* began. By June, the nine judges ruled eight to one that the taking of the Black Hills was unfair and ordered the U.S.

government to pay for the land they had taken. The price for the Black Hills was set at $17.5 million, plus millions of dollars more in interest. Since the decision, the Sioux have refused the money, saying that they only want their land back. In 1999, President Bill Clinton visited the Pine Ridge Reservation in the first nation-to-nation meeting in more than fifty years. He told listeners, "We're not coming from Washington to tell you exactly what to do and how to do it, we're coming from Washington to ask you what you want to do, and tell you we will give you the tools and the support to get done what you want to do for your children and their future." Ceremonial chief Frank Fools Crow of the Teton Sioux said, "The survival of the world depends upon our sharing what we have and working together." And so South Dakotans have entered the twenty-first century with shared challenges and new visions.

President Bill Clinton meets with Sioux natives on the Pine Ridge Reservation. Clinton was the first U.S. president to visit a reservation in more than fifty years.

Important Dates

10,000–8,000 B.C.E. Prehistoric humans hunt mammoth and bison, using stone weapons.

500 C.E. Mound Builders settle in villages along the Missouri River.

1600s Arikara tribe builds villages and trades horses for trade goods.

1743 La Vérendrye brothers explore and claim area for France.

1760-1794 Sioux migrate onto the plains, driving Arikara north.

1803 President Jefferson purchases the Louisiana Territory from France.

1804, 1806 The Lewis and Clark expedition travels along the Missouri River through Dakota Territory.

1817 Joseph La Framboise establishes a fur trading post and the first permanent white settlement in South Dakota, near Fort Pierre.

Sitting Bull

1861 Congress creates the Dakota Territory.

1862 Congress passes the Homestead Act.

1868 The Fort Laramie Treaty is signed, establishing the Great Sioux Reservation which includes the Black Hills.

1874 The gold rush to the Black Hills begins. As a result, miners and Sioux clash.

1877 The U.S. government takes control of the Black Hills.

1890 Hundreds of Native American men, women, and children are killed during the Wounded Knee Massacre.

1927 Gutzon Borglum begins carving Mount Rushmore.

1930s The dust bowl era and Great Depression hit Dakota farmers hard.

1944-1960s Missouri River dams projects provide jobs and wealth for the state.

1973 The American Indian Movement members hold a political stand-off at Wounded Knee.

1980 Supreme Court rules that U.S. government must pay back the Sioux for having taken the Black Hills.

1990 Near Faith, South Dakota, fossil hunter Sue Hendrickson discovers the largest and most complete *T. Rex* ever found.

"Sue" the T. rex

2001 U.S. senator Tom Daschle of South Dakota becomes the U.S. Senate majority leader.

3 The People

Whether exploring South Dakota by foot, canoe, horseback, wagon, steamboat, train, automobile, motorcycle, or bicycle, travelers have always found plenty of places to stop and marvel. Millions have made their way, one way or another, across the state, and hundreds of thousands have chosen to call it home.

> The official state greeting is borrowed from the Lakota language. "Hau, Kola!" means "Hello, Friend!"

Settling In

For more than a century, the Arikara Indians had South Dakota to themselves. In the mid-1700s, French trappers, traders, and missionaries passed through, sometimes pausing to set up a trading post, or convert the native people to Catholicism. At about the same time, the Sioux had begun their migration into the territory. Before long, the area was the center of the richest period of Plains Indian culture. Deeply tied to the land, the Plains tribes rejoiced in its bounty. There was water, food, and shelter for all. As Lakota chief Red Cloud described, "The Great

Many South Dakota farms have been run by the same family for generations.

41

Spirit made us, the Indians, and gave us this land we live in. He gave us the buffalo, the antelope, and the deer for food and clothing. . . . We were free as the winds. . . ”

Though the first Europeans to settle the region were French, most left once the trade in beaver pelts had ended. But farmers from the East soon arrived leading their ox-driven wagons onto their new prairie farms. In the late 1800s, European immigrants joined in the Dakota homestead boom. And when gold was discovered in the Black Hills, a new breed of adventure-seekers also moved in.

The diversity of people that has come together on this land is colorfully reflected in the names of their counties and communities. Miners and other fortune-hunters settled into towns they called Deadwood, Lead, and Shirttail Canyon. The state capital bears a Frenchman's name, Pierre (though it is pronounced "peer"). Many places were named in honor of the European cities left behind by immigrant pioneers. Some examples are Bristol (England), Vienna (Austria), Stockholm (Sweden), and Tabor (in what is now the Czech Republic). There were also "back home" communities on the East Coast, such as Arlington (Virginia) and Amherst (Massachusetts). Throughout the state, you see Native American names such as Oahe (a Sioux word meaning "something to stand on"), Oglala (a branch of the Teton Sioux), or Minnehaha (Sioux word meaning "falling water," or "waterfall"). The state itself is named after the Dakota tribe whose name means "an alliance of friends."

A Wealth of Traditions

A little less than 90 percent of South Dakotans today are white. Most of them are English, German, Irish, French,

Russian, Portuguese, Scandanavian, or Czech. Many are related to the early homesteading families. About 63,000 Native Americans, which is 8 percent of the total population, live in the state. Many of these Native Americans live on one of the state's nine reservations. Slightly more than 1.5 percent of the population is Latino. Asians and African-American residents each make up fewer than 1 percent of the population.

The nine reservations within South Dakota are Cheyenne River, Crow Creek, Flandreau Santee, Lake Traverse Sisseton, Lower Brule, Pine Ridge, Rosebud, Standing Rock, and Yankton.

Children often care for farm animals and do chores around the farm.

Each of these many different ethnic groups has added to the state's culture. Through the many ethnic traditions, customs, foods, songs, stories, and festivals, South Dakota's rich heritage emerges. Czechs celebrate Tabor Days with polka dances, ethnic costumes, and a delicious pastry called a *kolache*. When Swedes near Sioux Falls gather for holidays, several appetizers are spread out in a style known as a smorgasbord. Norwegians celebrate Norway's Independence Day on May 17 each year with parades, games, sports, and picnics. People of German-Russian background hold a German Schmeckfest in Eureka featuring sausage making, basket weaving, songfests, pioneer demonstrations, and healthy servings of a coffee cake called *kuchen*.

These South Dakotans are dressed for the Czech Fest in Tabor.

Recipe for *Kuchen*

Kuchen is a tasty German cake and is the state's official dessert. There are as many recipes for *kuchen* as there are good cooks in South Dakota. You can make *kuchen* with cherries, berries, plums, peaches, cheese, or raisins. Try this recipe for blueberry *kuchen*.

Ingredients:

For the crust you will need:
1 stick unsalted butter
1/4 cup sugar
1-1/2 cup flour
1/2 teaspoon salt
1 teaspoon vanilla
1 teaspoon baking powder
1 egg

To make the filling, you will need:
2 pints of blueberries (4-1/2 cups)
1/2 cup sugar
1 tablespoon cinnamon

Preheat the oven to 350 degrees Fahrenheit. Ask an adult to help you with the oven. While the oven is heating up, mix together the butter and sugar with an electric mixer. Add the rest of the crust ingredients and mix just until the dough is crumbly, but still holds together. Spread a coating of butter or margarine on the sides and bottom of a 9-inch pan. Then press the dough into the pan and up against the sides.

    Wash the berries and spread them on the dough. Gently press the berries into the dough. Sprinkle with cinnamon and sugar. Bake at 350 degrees F for 25 to 35 minutes, until the crust turns golden brown. Remove from the oven and set out to cool. If you like, you can enjoy your kuchen *with a big scoop of vanilla ice cream.*

The Germans, French, and Irish brought the Catholic religion to the state, while the Scandanavians brought their Lutheran faith. One of the most famous events in South Dakota is the Black Hills Passion Play, which reenacts the Easter story of Jesus Christ. Native Americans uphold their heritage at the many powwows and events held on their reservations. At powwows, some ceremonies are religious, such as the Sun Dance and the naming ceremony. In other events, men, women, and children take part in dance competitions, such as the grass dance, the fancy dance, or the jingle dress dance, as well as traditional activities such as storytelling and the gift-

giving "giveaway." Traditional foods are also enjoyed, such as buffalo stew, tripe, fry bread, and *wojopi*, a type of pudding.

Although ethnic traditions run strong in South Dakota, other celebrations show off the state's unique charm. In Mitchell, a Russian-inspired building called the Corn Palace was erected to honor farmers and their harvest. Each year, during the harvest festival, fantastic murals made of corn and wheat grass decorate the Corn Palace inside and out.

A boy dances at a traditional Lakota Wacipi, *or powwow.*

These South Dakotans enjoy the fireworks at a Fort Pierre rodeo.

Rodeos, roundups, stampedes, and historical cavalry reenactments are ways South Dakotans display their western frontier heritage. The colorful history of the Black Hills is played out each year in festivities such as '76 Miners Days, the Cowboy Poetry Gathering, Native American Day at the Crazy Horse Memorial, and the world-famous Sturgis motorcycle rally and races.

The Crazy Horse Volksmarch is an event held in the Black Hills that attracts thousands of visitors from around the world each year. A volksmarch is a large, organized hike. The story behind this celebration began in 1939, when Lakota official Standing Bear asked Polish sculptor Korczak Ziolkowski to carve an image of Chief Crazy Horse. He said, "My fellow chiefs and I would like the white man to know the [Native American] man has great heroes too." Standing Bear and

This is a model of the Crazy Horse Memorial with the unfinished memorial behind it.

Ziolkowski chose a site not far from Mount Rushmore in the Black Hills. Ziolkowski believed in the project so much that he invested his own money. In 1947, he began blasting millions of tons of rock from the 6,741-foot granite peak. The sculptor did not live to see his project completed, so after his death his family vowed to complete the monument. Once a year, visitors are offered an up-close view of the work-in-progress. During the volksmarch, they climb the 741 steps up to the 600-foot carving of Crazy Horse, the world's largest sculpture.

Near and Far

"The whole of South Dakota is one big small town," says a rancher from Echo Valley. Population numbers are proof of that. The United States averages about 80 people per square mile. This is much higher than South Dakota's average of just 9 people per square mile. South Dakota has one of the highest rural populations in the country. Half of the state's citizens live in these communities.

Only the state's largest city, Sioux Falls, has more than 100,000 people. Rapid City is next with close to 55,000. After that, the populations of other cities are much smaller. Vermillion, with a population of around 10,000, is home to the University of South Dakota. People in town were very surprised and excited when an article about the good life in Vermillion appeared in the newspaper, *The Wall Street Journal.* Community leaders boasted about the article in a local newspaper, "In Vermillion the cost of living is affordable, there is low crime, good education, good climate, a good work force . . ." Residents in other parts of the state report that living in a small city or town in South Dakota gives you choices. There are many theaters, parks, galleries, and museums to visit, such as the Museum of Geology, Oscar Howe Art Center, Black Hills Mining Museum, or South Dakota Air & Space Museum. Or you can head for the "wide open spaces" and enjoy nature and the outdoors.

The city of Sioux Falls was settled in 1865, near the falls of the Big Sioux River.

Famous South Dakotans

Crazy Horse: Native American Leader

Crazy Horse was a nineteenth-century Oglala Lakota chief. Widely admired for his bravery and skill in combat, he led Sioux warriors to victory in the battle of Little Big Horn. Afterwards, in the winter of 1877, American soldiers attacked and surrounded his camp. When his followers began to starve, Crazy Horse surrendered. The American soldiers put him in prison. Later, when they suspected he was trying to escape, they killed him. Today, visitors can view the Crazy Horse Memorial near Custer, South Dakota.

Tom Brokaw: Journalist

Tom Brokaw is the anchor of the NBC Nightly News. He was born in 1940 on a farm in Webster, South Dakota. He worked for a local radio station and married Miss South Dakota, his high school sweetheart. After studying political science at the University of South Dakota, he became a television news reporter. Throughout his career, he has traveled widely to report on major world events and to interview many world leaders.

Russell Means: Activist

Russell Means, an Oglala Lakota, was born in 1939 on the Pine Ridge Indian Reservation. Since the 1960s he has been a leading spokesperson for American Indian rights. As the first director of the American Indian Movement (AIM), he led demonstrations at Alcatraz Island, Plymouth Rock, and Wounded Knee. These brought worldwide attention to the poverty and injustice that American Indians suffer. He is also an actor and an author.

Tom Daschle: Politician

Senator Tom Daschle was born in 1947, in Aberdeen, South Dakota. After graduating from the University of South Dakota with a degree in political science, he served in the U.S. Air Force. In 1976, he was elected to the U.S. House of Representatives and later, to the U.S. Senate. As the senior senator and majority leader of the 107th Congress, he became a major national figure. But Daschle never forgets that he is from South Dakota. Each year, the Senator drives through all sixty-six counties and stops wherever people are gathered. At fairs, meetings, auctions, health clinics, clubs, or schools he talks with his fellow South Dakotans.

Vera Cleaver: Writer

In 1919, Vera Allen was born in the tiny town of Virgil. She started writing at the age of six. Once she met her husband, Bill Cleaver, they formed a husband-and-wife writing team. They wrote hundreds of articles, short stories, and novels. After he died, she continued to write and her books were often included on the lists of outstanding books for young people. The Cleavers created young characters who faced the hardships of rural life with courage and dignity. Some of the books, such as Sweetly Sings the Donkey *and* Dust of the Earth, *were set in South Dakota.*

Billy Mills: Athlete

Billy Mills, whose Oglala Sioux name is "Loves His Country," was born on the Pine Ridge Reservation. At the Haskell Indian College and later at the University of Kansas, Mills trained as a runner and was part of a winning track-and-field team. After serving in the Marines, he qualified for the 10,000-meter race at the 1964 summer Olympics in Tokyo. On the day of the race, Mills ran his best, beating some of the world's fastest runners.

Historic buildings are preserved at Prairie Village, a museum of small-town pioneer life.

Friends and Neighbors

While South Dakota communities are close knit, they do have their share of problems. Farming and ranch life are difficult ways to make a living. Most young people no longer want to live on a remote farm. Many small towns are losing their younger residents to bigger cities. "Most of our towns are really just retirement towns," says one lifelong resident. The same problem also exists on the reservations. Unemployment, poverty, sickness, and a lack of opportunities make reservation life a challenge for some. When Native American students leave the reservation for college, they seldom return. People shake their heads sadly when they think about the new ideas and technical skills their young people could bring to their communities, if they only came back home. "It's hard these days," says one resident. "You don't want to get stale, you have to be creative to make it all work, or you will lose it!"

One young Oglala woman was very creative in her short life. SuAnne Big Crow played basketball on the Pine Ridge high school team, the Lady Thorpes. She was loved not only for her athletic skills, but for her kindness. After graduating, she planned to go to college and return to Pine Ridge, to help her people.

One night, she became a hero to many more than the people of Pine Ridge. The Lady Thorpes were preparing to play the Lead High School team. Before the game, the people in the gym began to call out war whoops and other taunts that mocked the Indian team. The Lady Thorpes' captain was afraid to leave the locker room and face the jeering crowd. So SuAnne said she would go. She stood in the center of that big, unfriendly gymnasium and bowed her head. Then she removed her warm-up jacket and used it to perform a traditional shawl dance. The crowd grew quiet and before long, they understood SuAnne's proud act of courage. Soon, everyone began to cheer. The Lady Thorpes won the game, and went on to tour Europe. Tragically, SuAnne was killed in an automobile accident, but her vision for Pine Ridge lives on. Her dream of a "rainbow place" where children on the reservation can play safely is now a reality. The SuAnne Big Crow Boys' and Girls' Club of Pine Ridge is an exciting example of South Dakotans of all ages working together to build stronger communities.

Calendar of Events

Czech Days in Tabor
Every June, thousands of people come to Tabor to celebrate Czech heritage. They enjoy parades, polka music, traditional costumes, dances, and the tasty Czech pastry, *kolache*.

Sioux Tribe Annual Wacipi
The "powwow season" runs from March through September. The Sisseton-Wahpeton *wacipi* is the oldest powwow in South Dakota. For more than a century, the tribe has gathered in Agency Village to sing, dance, pray, honor friendships, and feast together.

The Laura Ingalls Wilder Pageant
In July, tourists visit De Smet for a taste of the pioneer experience. Actors re-create scenes from the author's *Little House on the Prairie* books, near the site of Ma and Pa Ingalls's original homestead.

The South Dakota State Fair
Many South Dakotans plan their summer vacations in late July and early August so that they can go to the state fair. The event is loaded with agricultural and craft exhibits, livestock shows, rodeos, car races, farm machinery displays, carnival rides, and more.

The Laura Ingalls Wilder Pageant

Lewis and Clark Festival

Every year on August 25, the community of Vermillion commemorates the day the Lewis and Clark expedition reached the local landmark known as Spirit Mound— August 25, 1804.

Sturgis Motorcycle Rally and Races

Each August, hundreds of thousands of motorcycle riders rev up their engines and gather in the small mountain town of Sturgis for races and lively celebrations.

The German-Russian Schmeckfest

This September celebration in Eureka honors the heritage of the German-Russian immigrants who long ago left Russia for the windswept prairies of South Dakota. The Schmeckfest activities include music, dance, and traditional foods.

Corn Palace Harvest Festival

In late summer, South Dakotans decorate the Corn Palace in Mitchell with murals made of corn and wheat. They celebrate their harvest with live entertainment, food, carnival rides, and a rodeo.

Frontier Christmas at Fort Sisseton

Visitors step back in time to celebrate an old-fashioned Christmas at one of the best-preserved forts of the American frontier. Activities include prairie crafts, food, storytelling, music, and sleigh rides

Mitchell Corn Palace

4 How It Works

There are many levels of government in South Dakota: county, municipal, state, tribal, and federal. The state is divided into sixty-six counties. South Dakota voters elect commissioners to run county governments. Mayors or councils are elected to run municipal governments in cities, towns, or villages. There are more than three hundred such municipalities in the state. Each reservation has a tribal government. Leaders are elected to tribal councils. At the level of state government, voters elect legislators, a governor, and other executive office holders. For representation in the federal government, South Dakotans elect two senators and one member to the House of Representatives.

Making Laws

In 1898, less than ten years after gaining statehood, South Dakota citizens were the first in the country to decide on a method of lawmaking called initiative and referendum. In an initiative, people sign a petition asking for a certain law to be created. If enough people vote for the initiative on Election

Mount Rushmore, with its patriotic images of Presidents Washington, Jefferson, Roosevelt, and Lincoln, is a popular destination for tourists.

Day, then it becomes a law without having to pass through the legislature or be signed by the governor. In a referendum, people sign a petition asking that an existing law be changed or removed. If enough people vote for the referendum, then the existing law is changed or struck down. To this day, South Dakota voters set an example for other states with this system. Not all states allow this process. And some states that do have had serious problems, such as creating laws that harm the state economy. But South Dakotans choose their petitions wisely. As a senator from neighboring Minnesota told voters, "I've seen first hand how well this can work. South Dakotans have taken this responsibility very seriously, using it sparingly and sensibly."

Although laws can be adopted by initiative, most laws in South Dakota are created by the legislature. Some bills begin in the house of representatives, and others begin in the senate. In either case, the methods are similar. To begin, a legislator with an idea for a law suggests, or drafts, a bill. Later, he or she presents the bill to the bill clerk. After the clerk gives the bill a number, the process is under way. Next, the chief clerk reads the bill out loud. After the reading, an officer assigns the bill to a committee. There are many committees and each focuses on a certain subject such as agriculture, education, natural resources, health, commerce, transportation, or taxes. Copies of the bill are printed and given to committee members and any other interested citizen. Committee meetings are open to the public. During the meetings, members review the bill and listen to people who have come to talk about why they are in favor of, or why they oppose, the bill. If the committee approves the bill, the next day it is read out loud a second time to the entire house.

The capitol is an elegant building made of sandstone, limestone, and marble, set on a foundation of South Dakota granite.

Branches of Government

Executive The governor is the chief officer of the executive branch. He or she is the head of the state and is elected to a four-year term and may only serve two terms in a row. The duties of the governor include preparing the state budget, suggesting new laws, and selecting important officials. He or she must also sign bills into law or reject them, which is called a veto.

Legislative The legislative branch is made up of thirty-five senators and seventy representatives. Voters in each of the thirty-five districts can cast their ballots for one senator and two representatives. Members of the legislature meet each year in the state capital, Pierre. When they are not in session, they have other occupations, such as farmer, teacher, lawyer, surgeon, or homemaker.

Judicial The judicial branch is a system of courts made up of the supreme court, circuit courts, and lower courts, called magistrate courts. The highest court in the state is the supreme court. It consists of a chief justice and four associate justices who are first appointed by the governor and later reelected by voters. The justices oversee other courts and rule on the most important cases. Circuit courts are the general trial courts that make decisions on serious crimes and lawsuits. The lower courts rule on small claims and lesser crimes such as traffic violations.

This is when other members can debate and suggest changes to the bill. Once the exact wording of the bill is decided, a vote is taken. If a majority votes in favor, then the bill moves on to the other legislative body. If they also vote in favor, then the bill is delivered to the governor. If the governor signs the bill, it becomes law. If the governor refuses to sign, it is vetoed, or rejected. If the bill is vetoed, it is returned to the legislature.

The members of the legislature must then decide whether to overturn the governor's veto. Two-thirds of both houses must vote in favor of the bill to reverse the veto and allow the bill to become law.

Everyone Has a Voice

South Dakotans strongly believe that every person's voice counts. In the election of November 1998, the majority of voters in South Dakota passed a referendum called Amendment E. This referendum banned large corporations from operating certain kinds of farms in South Dakota. Amendment E became a part of the state constitution. There have been court challenges to this change. But since the 1974 "Family Farm Act"— which recognizes the importance of family farms and the threat made to them by corporate farming—South Dakotans have voted to fend off large corporate farms. Ninety-four percent of the land in South Dakota is devoted to agriculture, and it is home to about 35,000 farms. Family farmers and ranchers say the profits from large-scale corporate farms end up in corporate headquarters and not in the local economy. South Dakota farmers have a long history of independence, and the idea of working their own land to benefit a distant corporation sends many voters to the polls. As rancher Ron Ogren commented, "It's important to be aware of what we can do to help ourselves." So with the power of the right to vote, South Dakota's citizens do exactly that.

In 1992, some schools chose to start a Kids Voting Day. By the year 2000, more than 75,000 South Dakota students took part in the event. Kids Voting Day is a program in the schools for students from kindergarten through high school.

South Dakotans gather at the state capital to express their opinions.

Students study the way government works, read about and debate the political issues of the day. Finally, on Election Day, they go with their parents to real polling places and cast their votes. The students' votes are published in the next day's newspapers. Lawmakers believe the program helps everyone.

Students learn they are an important part of the election process. And after students get involved at school, many go home and talk about the issues with their families and encourage their parents to vote. In 2002, the legislature called the program a success saying, "The need for Kids Voting is greater now than ever because we must make every effort . . . to educate our students about why it is so important to be active citizens, to be involved in their communities, to play active roles, and use their votes and their voices. . ."

**To contact South Dakota's governor
go to this Web site:
http://www.state.sd.us/governor/index.htm
To find South Dakota's state legislators go to this Web site:
http://legis.state.sd.us
The quickest way to look up telephone numbers, addresses, and email of
your U.S. legislators is to type in your zip code on this Web site:
http://www.congress.org**

5 Making a Living

The Missouri River does more than split South Dakota through the middle. It divides the way citizens make a living. As author John Steinbeck wrote in *Travels with Charley,* "The two sides of the river might well be a thousand miles apart." East River, as the land east of the Missouri River is called, is rolling farmland dotted with small cities and towns. Communities are more closely spaced, farms are smaller, and the population there is greater. West River, on the other hand, is dry and rugged. People and towns are farther apart in this land of cattle ranches, windmills, badlands, mountain ranges, and distant towns.

Farming

No matter which side of the divide South Dakotans live on, they live close to the land. As one East River farmer boasted, "My great grandfather farmed when grasses were as tall as a horse's ear!" Farmers now grow rows of sunflowers, flax, hay, rye, and corn, as well as dairy cattle and poultry. Nearly

Outdoor activities, such as horseback riding, are a treasured part of living in South Dakota.

On the family farm everybody lends a hand.

one in ten persons in South Dakota works in agriculture. Farmers are proud of their heritage and their family's ties to the land, but it is becoming more and more of a struggle to afford to operate a farm. Farmers say it takes 3,000 to 4,000 acres to support one family. Crops need rain. South Dakota's unreliable rainfall, plus the high cost of farm machinery, supplies, taxes, and land, means that farmers are forced to find other ways to pay the bills. Modern equipment is another added expense. Many of today's farmers have a computer in the tractor cab where they can download satellite photos that track crops growing in the fields and the movements of livestock. Said one farming couple, "It's not for the faint of heart, this lifestyle, but it's worth all the challenges and high blood pressure!"

City Life

Sioux Falls, and other cities east of the river, such as Brookings, Yankton, Mitchell, and Vermillion, offer many different ways to make a living. There, the unemployment rate is very low. These cities offer jobs in manufacturing food products, farm equipment, tools, and machinery. People can also find jobs in technology fields such as computers and telecommunications.

Colleges and universities are an important part of eastern South Dakota cities. Most workers in South Dakota have a job in a service industry such as health care, retail, entertainment, publishing, or banking. Pierre, the capital, is located in the center of the state. Workers there hold jobs in government and other service fields.

At the state's universities, students join scientists in researching better ways to grow corn and other crops.

Products & Resources

Seeds and Grains

Plenty of sun and enough water help make South Dakota the second-largest producer of flax and sunflower seeds in the nation. It is the third-largest producer of hay and rye.

Bees and Honey

For the last decade, South Dakota has been a national leader in honey production. The state has produced more than 20 million pounds of honey from nearly 250,000 hives. The honeybee is the South Dakota state insect and usually makes its sweet-tasting honey from a blend of clover and alfalfa.

Granite

Granite outcroppings in South Dakota were formed during the age of glaciers. Today, the state is one of the leading producers of granite. More than 650,000 tons a year of a beautiful, deep red granite, called mahogany granite, are mined and prized around the world. It is used in floor tiles, counter tops, and monuments.

Waterpower

The Oahe Dam on the Missouri River is the fourth-largest manmade dam in the United States. At 242 feet high and 9,360 feet long, the Oahe Dam produces electricity for South Dakota and four neighboring states.

Manufacturing

A wide range of products are made throughout the state. This includes medical equipment, computers, computer parts, and the electronic scoreboards seen in sports stadiums.

Tourism

Visitors to South Dakota mean big business to the state. Tourists bring in more than a billion dollars each year. Attractions include Mount Rushmore, the Badlands, Crazy Horse National Monument, Wind Cave National Park, and the Black Hills.

Buffalo cross a road at Custer State Park. The American buffalo is slowly making a comeback.

Western Resources

On the West River side, ranchers raise herds of beef cattle and buffalo on dry, scrub grass rangelands. While cattle ranching is big business on the Great Plains, raising buffalo is a small but growing trend. Buffalo meat is rich in protein and low in fat. Many believe that the source of the Plains Indians' amazing strength as warriors and hunters was due in large part to a diet of this meat. Today, there are herds grazing on public lands such as Custer State Park and Wind Cave National Park and on all of South Dakota's tribal lands. The country's largest herds can be found on three private South Dakota ranches.

Along with raising buffalo, farming, and ranching, residents of South Dakota's Indian reservations are finding new ways to build up their economy. Many work in gaming casinos run by the tribes. Casinos provide a new source of income for the tribes. On the Rosebud Sioux Reservation, tribal members are building a wind farm. The high-tech wind turbine has three large blades and stands on a hill where winds average 18 miles per hour. Organizers expect the wind farm will produce enough electricity for two hundred homes each year.

In the Badlands and the Black Hills, workers take on many different types of jobs. They are park rangers, forest workers, loggers, mill workers, miners, cowboys, tour guides, and geologists, just to name a few. Though only 3 percent of South Dakota is forested. Loggers have been cutting billions of board feet of Ponderosa pine and white spruce in the Black Hills since 1899. And as soon as General George Custer reported, "Gold has been found," the cities of Deadwood and Lead have been home to mine workers. However, the Homestake Mine in Lead, which was one of the nation's largest gold mines for more than a century, has

closed. People in Lead hope the mine—with its many elevators and shaft systems—will be remade into a large underground national science laboratory.

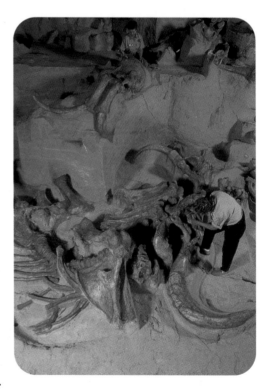

Because there are fewer people in western South Dakota, there are fewer cities. Rapid City is the largest and is a regional center for a large part of the Great Plains. Residents of Wyoming, Nebraska, Colorado, and Montana come to Rapid City for entertainment, supplies, health care, and other needs. The South Dakota School of Mines and Technology in Rapid City is a center for engineering and the study of geology. Scientists, rock hounds, and

Paleontologists unearth mammoth remains from a site in Hot Springs.

archaeologists have long been drawn to the area's incredible fossils and rock samples. Several important fossils have been discovered in the region.

In 1990, while digging for fossils near Faith, South Dakota, Susan Hendrickson discovered the largest and most complete *Tyrannosaurus rex* skeleton ever found. The dinosaur is named Sue in her honor. It is on display at the Field Museum of Natural History in Chicago.

Tourism is a fast-growing state industry. Most tourists head for the western portion of the state, seeking historic sites, outdoor recreation, nature, wildlife, and spectacular scenery in the Black Hills, Badlands National Park, Custer State Park, Wind Cave National Park, Mount Rushmore, and the Crazy Horse National Monument. Mount Rushmore has been a very popular destination, especially after the terrorist attacks in 2001, as record-breaking numbers of tourists have come to show their patriotism and national pride. Travelers on the road to Mount Rushmore will see countless signs along the route, promising "Free Ice Water" at Wall Drug. Once a tiny drugstore in a town forgotten during the Great Depression, Wall Drugstore's owners posted road signs advertising free ice water. Soon tourists came in droves, drank the ice water, and bought souvenirs. Wall Drug now takes up most of the town and features restaurants, dozens of shops, and of course, free ice water.

The former Black Hills mining town of Deadwood has also looked to tourism to keep its economy healthy. With nearly all of the mines shut down, the community remade itself into a "wild west" town featuring gambling casinos and reenactments of the lives of famous gold-rush characters such as Wild Bill Hickok and Calamity Jane. Another town, Spearfish, attracts hunters, hikers, river rafters, and fishermen from all over the country, while each

The 1876 gold rush is an ongoing source of pride for the city of Deadwood.

year the nearby town of Sturgis hosts hundreds of thousands of motorcycle riders in the world famous Sturgis Motor-cycle Rally and Races.

The Big Muddy

The 2,500-mile Missouri River has always been important to the state's history. In 1804, Lewis and Clark marveled at the so-called Big Muddy. They also drew and observed many formerly unknown plants and animals found along its banks. A hundred years later, writer George Fitch called the river "tawny, restless, brawling."

Once the pioneers settled along the river, they put it to work for them. The river fed their crops, powered their machinery, and transported their supplies. But the river also flooded their fields and homes, washed away riverbanks, and formed sandbars that damaged and wrecked boats. By the 1960s, dams had been built. They prevented floods, slowed soil erosion, made electricity from waterpower, and created navigation channels for barges to pass. They also formed four large reservoirs known as the Great Lakes of South Dakota. These lakes provide recreational activities such as boating, swimming, and fishing. But today, many say that the Missouri River is one of the country's most endangered rivers. Author Stephen Ambrose said, "The river has been damaged. . . . It's a great big ditch."

The Missouri River winds its way through the heart of South Dakota, passing through Pierre.

Citizens are hoping to change that. They say that there are other ways to run the dams that will help the economy and restore the river to its former "tawny, restless, brawling" self. By making the river cleaner and healthier for fish and wildlife, the state will earn more money from increased tourism. Senator Tom Daschle praises the efforts of South Dakotans for their care and concern for their environment. "I'm fortunate to represent South Dakota," he said, "a state blessed with great natural beauty. We are home to vast farmland, the majestic Missouri River, the stark and beautiful Badlands, and the dense forest of the Black Hills. We know how important it is to be good stewards of our land, water and air." With the help of new technology, fresh ideas, and a willingness to work hard, South Dakotans have much to look forward to. As South Dakota pioneer and novelist, Ole Rolvaag, described in his book, *Giants in the Earth*, South Dakotans can see a "bright, clear sky, today, tomorrow, and for all time to come."

The state flag of South Dakota is sky blue with the great seal of South Dakota in the center. South Dakota, the Mount Rushmore State, is printed around the seal.

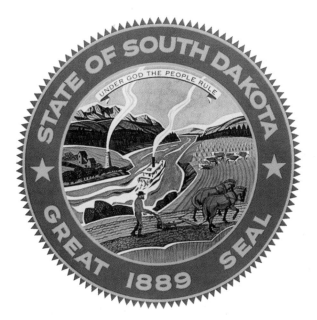

On a blue background, the seal features golden circles surrounding a farmer plowing with a team of horses. There is a field with cattle, a steamboat going upriver past a smoking mill, and hills in the distance. The words in the seal declare, "Under God the People Rule." The year of statehood, 1889, is included.

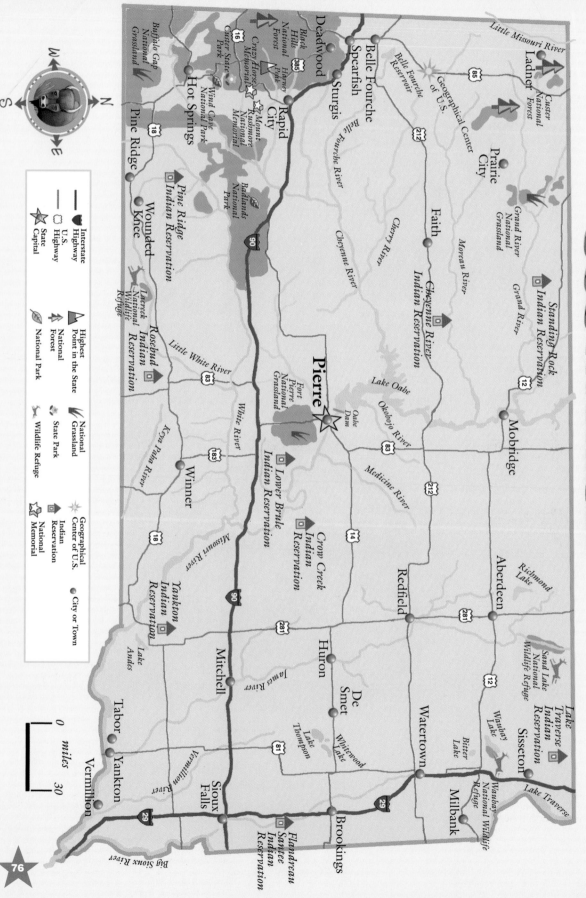

SOUTH DAKOTA

Map legend:
- Interstate Highway
- U.S. Highway
- State Capital
- Highest Point in the State
- National Forest
- National Park
- National Grassland
- State Park
- Wildlife Refuge
- Geographical Center of U.S.
- Indian Reservation
- National Memorial
- City or Town

Compass: N, S, E, W

Scale: 0 miles 30

Little Missouri River

Ladner

Buffalo Gap National Grassland

Custer National Forest

Black Hills National Forest

Deadwood

Spearfish

Belle Fourche

Sturgis

Belle Fourche Reservoir

Belle Fourche River

Geographical Center of U.S.

Crazy Horse Memorial

Harney Peak

Rapid City

Mount Rushmore National Memorial

Custer State Park

Wind Cave National Park

Hot Springs

Pine Ridge

Wounded Knee

Pine Ridge Indian Reservation

Badlands National Park

Prairie City

Grand River National Grassland

Grand River

Standing Rock Indian Reservation

Faith

Moreau River

Cheyenne River

Cherry River

Cheyenne River Indian Reservation

Mobridge

Lake Oahe

Okobojo River

Oahe Dam

Pierre

Fort Pierre National Grassland

Medicine River

Little White River

Rosebud Indian Reservation

Lacreek National Wildlife Refuge

Keya Paha River

White River

US 83

US 183

Winner

US 18

Lower Brule Indian Reservation

Crow Creek Indian Reservation

Redfield

Aberdeen

Richmond Lake

Sand Lake National Wildlife Refuge

Lake Traverse Indian Reservation

Sisseton

Waubay National Wildlife Refuge

Waubay Lake

Bitter Lake

Lake Traverse

Milbank

Watertown

De Smet

Huron

Whitewood Lake

James River

Lake Thompson

Brookings

Flandreau Santee Indian Reservation

Sioux Falls

Mitchell

Lake Andes

Yankton Indian Reservation

Missouri River

Tabor

Yankton

Vermillion

Vermillion River

Big Sioux River

I-90

I-29

US 81

US 281

US 212

US 14

US 16

US 385

US 85

US 212

US 12

US 83

Hail! South Dakota

Words and Music by Deecort Hammitt

Hail! South Da - ko - ta, A great state of the land, _____ Health, wealth and beau - ty, That's what makes her grand; _____ She has her Black Hills, And mines with gold so rare, _____ And with her scen' - ry, No state can com - pare. _____

State Song

More About South Dakota

Books

Bial, Raymond. *The Sioux*. New York: Benchmark Books, 1999.

Bruchac, Joseph. *Crazy Horse's Vision*. New York: Lee & Low Books, 2000.

Curlee, Lynn. *Rushmore*. New York: Scholastic Press, 1999.

Freedman, Russell. *Buffalo Hunt*. New York: Holiday House, 1988.

Left Hand Bull, Jacqueline. *Lakota Hoop Dancer*. New York: Dutton Children's Books, 1999.

Robinson, Fay. *A Dinosaur Named Sue: The Find of the Century*. New York: Scholastic, 1999.

Waldman, Neil. *Wounded Knee*. New York: Atheneum Books for Young Readers, 2001.

Web Sites

Official South Dakota Government Web site:

http://www.state.sd.us

Wind Cave National Park:

http://www.wind.cave.national-park.com

About the Author

Ruth Bjorklund lives on Bainbridge Island, a ferry ride away from Seattle, Washington, with her husband, two children, two dogs, and three cats. In researching South Dakota, she has made some fascinating discoveries and some wonderful new friends.

Index

Page numbers in **boldface** are illustrations.